The 7 Secrets to Living with Joy and Riches

Also by Madeleine Kay

Living Serendipitously . . . keeping the wonder alive

Living with Outrageous Joy

Serendipitously Rich . . .
How to Get Delightfully, Delectably, Deliciously Rich
(or anything else you want) in 7 <u>Ridiculously</u> Easy Steps

The 12 Myths About Money

E-Books

~~Filthy~~ ~~Obscenely~~ Deliciously Rich . . .
How to Get Rich (or anything else you want)
in 6 Really Easy Steps

The 12 Myths About Money

Coming Soon

The UMM Factor . . .
(what you need in order to succeed)

How Will I Ever Get Over My Happy Childhood
(Short Stories)

The 7 Secrets to Living with Joy and Riches

Madeleine Kay

Published by

Chrysalis Publishing
P.O. Box 675
Flat Rock, NC 28731

ISBN 10: 0-9715572-0-9
ISBN 13: 978-0-9715572-0-8

Printed in the United States of America

"Joy is the most infallible sign of the presence of God."

– Pierre Tielhard de Chardin

DEDiCaTiON

To my parents – Harry and Anne Kay –
the richest people I have ever known.
They fill me . . . and everyone
who has ever known them
. . . with such joy.

Acknowledgements

To my son, Daniel, who is such a joy and enriches my life daily.

To my wonderful friends – Manuela Cobos, Yves Debarge, Renzo and Delores Favaretto, Randy Gilbert, Don Green, Fauna Hodel, Hope Marcus, Federico Velludo and Haze Wainberg – whose shining examples continually remind me what it means to live with joy and riches.

To my good friend and graphic designer, Claire Collins, whose friendship, support and computer assistance make this book possible.

To my dog and faithful companion, Yoda, whose *joie de vivre* is deliciously inspiring and reminds me to play.

To the creative impulse . . . that catapults me into a passion, an immediacy, a spontaneity that make writing come alive for me . . . and makes writing so much fun.

Note from the Author

I don't know when it happened, but somewhere in our history, we began to separate the joy and riches in our lives – joy had to do with non-material things, like nature, high ideals, friends, family, hobbies, ease and leisure . . . and riches had to do with work, struggle, effort, and material things and values.

Perhaps that was the moment when we truly began feeling separated from God – and lost our connection to the source of ALL there is . . . when we no longer associated joy, ease and beauty with the riches, abundance and prosperity we all desire – and that is our birthright.

And perhaps . . . that too is when so many of us stopped *wanting* those riches for ourselves – or at least, convinced ourselves we no longer wanted them or needed them. They seemed superfluous, somehow extraneous to what we truly valued . . . they seemed even, undesirable.

Have you ever noticed the words we use when referring to The Rich? "He's *filthy* rich" or "She's *obscenely* wealthy." We refer to money as "dirty" and people who care about or want or have money as greedy or selfish.

No wonder so many people don't have money and live in lack . . . and then wonder why! They don't *want* money. They don't want to be filthy, obscene, greedy or selfish.

But deep down – we all really *do* desire to be rich . . . to live richly and fully in every way, including money and wealth. And at some point in our lives, this desire rears its head and compels us to acknowledge it, to embrace it . . . and even . . . to rejoice in it . . . yes, to find joy in our desire and need for money and riches – to *savor* it . . . and to find it delightfully, delectably, deliciously exciting.

The seven secrets to living with joy and riches revealed in this book, will help *you* discover how to savor your life . . . not just work at . . . as you claim and enjoy all the joy and riches you desire.

"Riches do not consist in the possession of treasures, but in the use made of them."

— Napoleon Bonaparte

THE 7 SECRETS TO LIVING WITH JOY AND RICHES

INTRODUCTION

*"If you become whole,
everything will come to you."*

– Tao Te Ching

Respect money.

Appreciate joy.

And all the riches you desire

will come to you.

True wealth is the integration of body, mind and spirit.

Artistic creation has real value
and deserves to be compensated
just like any other job or
profession.

Living a rich and abundant life
is both noble and
desirable.

Claim your riches . . .
and reclaim your life.
Money and spirit are both the same . . .
they are all energy –
the currency of our lives.

Secret #1

DECIDE

"Be bold and mighty forces will come to your aid"

– Basil King

Decide to be rich
or anything else you want.
Don't just pray, hope,
plead or beg –
Decide . . .
Decide to do,
be or have
whatever you want . . .
and you will.

Commit yourself unwaveringly
to what you want . . .
And see the power that
doing so wields.

Everything changes
once you decide.
Your decision repositions you –
So your brain, your psyche,
begin to look
for ways for you
to get what you want –
rather
than wondering "if" you can.

Making a decision
catapults you into
the energy of possibility
where all things are possible . . .
because you have decided to
allow them to be –
you are inviting them into
your life and experience.

Making up your mind
to do something
is like the organizing principle
that allows everything to happen
and fall into place . . .
like a kaleidoscope
organizes the myriad pieces
inside into beautiful
and unique patterns.

Do . . . don't try!
Trying lacks energy –
It has no passion or commitment –
the two things that
are essential for
getting what you desire.

Announce that you
are ready to be
rich, happy, healthy, successful.
Do not ask – rather declare –
that you are ready to be rich,
willing to be happy . . .
that you have made
up your mind to be
healthy – and you will
succeed.

Know this –
once you make up your mind –
about anything . . . there is no
stopping you
because you strip yourself
and the situation down
to the bare essentials . . .
You distill everything
down to the
very core of what works,
what you need to do
to get whatever you want.

Once you make a firm,
unwavering decision to do,
be or have
whatever you want –
the " f " slips
out of the equation . . .
leaving only "when."

Secret # 2

Act

"What you can do, or dream you can, do it;
Boldness has genius, power and magic in it."

– Johann Wolfgang von Goethe

Do something . . . Anything!
Just get started.
Jump in and do it . . . do it now.

Jump in with both feet.
Seize the moment.
Take risks.
Dare to think big in
your pursuit of success.

Everything is connected
in the web of life.
If you just begin, if you act . . .
and keep on
"acting" and "doing,"
eventually you will wind up
where you want to be –
often even surpassing
your original vision.

Making a decision
to do something
points you in the right direction
and turns on your ignition . . .
Acting, or doing something,
puts you in gear.

Acting –
doing something –
is simple,
so don't complicate it.
Don't get stuck in your mind
with deliberations and procrastinations.
Just do it.

Action that is taken

in the moment,

while the spark

of enthusiasm is lit,

is fueled with a momentum

and propulsion

that action filtered

through the lens

of deliberation is not.

When you act on your decision
to do, be or have
whatever you want,
You must be ready to allow it . . .
willing to receive it.
Readiness is a threshold
upon which you stand . . .
a portal through
which you are ready to walk –
to claim what it is you desire.

Act and work smart, not hard.
Working smart is infinitely more
effective . . .
and a lot more satisfying
than working hard.

It is the passion, enthusiasm
and excitement
with which you act
that make you unstoppable.
They enable you to get more done
in a short period of time,
and to do it better,
more effectively,
efficiently and with
effortless ease . . .
and . . .
to even have fun while doing it.

Prosperity and abundance
are available to you –
you just need to be willing
and ready to tap into them . . .
willing to just *do* something . . .
anything . . .
to initiate the flow.

Acting, making one small

gesture, can

change everything.

The important thing is to act –

to *do* something –

which sets in motion

a chain of events that take on a life

of their own

. . . and you never know where they

will lead you.

When you act, always act
out of desire,
not need.
Need focuses on lack and what you
don't want.
Desire focuses on what
you *do* want
and
attracts it to you.

Secret # 3

Believe

"They can because they think they can."

– Virgil

Belief is that "thing,"
that "force" inside us –
that mental process infused
with faith and passion –
that makes all things possible
and real to us . . .
even when everything appears
to indicate the opposite.

Belief that is rooted in
passion and conviction
becomes a *knowing*.
It inhabits you so completely,
that the reality of it,
the accomplishment of it,
the "living" of it,
is never in question.

Unwavering belief radiates
out from the believer
and acts as a magnetic field
as well as a laser.
It magnetizes to you everything
and everyone you need
to achieve your desired goal . . .
while keeping you focused.

Full-bodied possibility living
is not just a mental attitude
that you have in your mind.
It is a belief that you "embody."
It lives and breathes in every cell
of your body,
so of course, it becomes a reality.

Unconditional belief
in getting what you want to do,
be or have
is like jet propulsion fuel –
it propels you
directly to your goal.

Be a visionary.
Be willing to go
beyond the boundaries
of the rational mind
that analyzes
and reacts to things
based on what it perceives
with our five senses.
Look to see
what is beyond the obvious.

With visioning, the result
or the end
becomes your starting point.
The result you desire becomes
so real for you –
that you already experience it
as a reality.
Then your daily life . . . just catches up
with that reality
that you are already living
and experiencing as real.

Your strong, unwavering belief creates
order out of chaos.
It creates the reality you want
and envision out of
a myriad of possible realities.

Expect what you want
and live as though
what you expect is on
its way to you.
You have to believe in miracles;
otherwise, they won't happen.
When you believe in them
and expect them –
you create a space for them
and invite them into your life.

Secret # 4

BE GRATEFUL

*"If the only prayer you said in your life
was 'Thank you,'
that would suffice."*

– Meister Eckhart

Gratitude is deep-rooted
and grows organically out of
who you are.
It is quite simply . . .
your response to being alive.

Gratitude is a quality of

your character –

one of your core values

that determines how you choose

to live every day.

Therefore,

it is totally within your control

rather than being

a capricious,

random reaction to life.

Gratitude is not reactive.
It does not need to wait
for someone or something
to act upon you
to set it in motion.
Gratitude is an attitude,
a way of living –
an active quality in and of itself.

Live with *active gratitude.*
Appreciate the small things.
Don't take anything for granted.
Do not overlook the "small" things for
"bigger" things that
seem more important.
They are not.

If you move through life
with *active gratitude*,
that responsiveness you
express to Life
creates, magnetizes, attracts
and elicits –
a responsiveness from Life
back to you.

Gratitude is active.

It is organic.

It can initiate a response.

Gratitude is imbued

with energy . . .

and therefore, functions according

to the laws of nature.

The energy flows to where
the attention goes.
When you are grateful,
energy flows to what you
are grateful for,
bringing more of what you
are grateful for
into your life.

Secret # 5

Rejoice

"Carpe diem! Rejoice while you are alive; enjoy the day; live life to the fullest; make the most of what you have."

— Horace, Ancient Roman Poet

Celebrate and rejoice in
your small accomplishments
on the way to your
larger goals.
This is not a luxury.
It's a necessity.

Experiencing
the thrill of accomplishment
along the way and not waiting until you
reach your goal –
helps you proceed and
continue moving
forward with gusto.

Rejoice in your small
successes.
This fills you with a sense
of satisfaction
that makes you feel complete –
and therefore,
whole and powerful.

Savoring your successes

energizes you –

and empowers you to

create even more success . . .

Savoring takes time . . .

it requires that

you relax . . . that you let go . . .

that you are fully present,

rather than thinking about what

you are going to do next.

Taking the time to savor
your small successes,
satiates you and fills you with
a sense of completion
so you can move
easily and fluidly
and totally on to the next thing.

To rejoice and celebrate
is a declaration of
unconditional trust
and thanksgiving . . .
and few things act more powerfully
than these two as a claim
upon the unseen forces
in the universe
to help you
get what you want.

When you rejoice,

you reconnect

with yourself,

with your source,

your core —

you reconnect with

why you do what you do . . .

with why you are alive —

for the sheer joy of it all.

When you rejoice, you are
making a declaration that
you are ready –
ready to succeed . . .
ready to be rich . . .
ready to be happy . . .
ready to love . . .
ready for whatever it is
you want to do next . . .
for whatever Life
wants to give you.

Secret # 6

Share

"We make a living by what we get,
but we make a life by what we give."

– Winston Churchill

The act of giving
touches some need in us –
a powerful desire
that is elemental and pure.

Sharing is something you do
not just because you are generous,
or because you are nice.
Sharing is something you do
because you cannot *not* do it.
It is compelling . . .
It is gratifying . . .
It is something you simply
have to do.

Largesse is . . .
"The joy of largeness;
great generosity; generosity
of spirit or attitude."
The largesse of philanthropy
is fluid – like a liquid
in which you can no longer
separate the various elements . . .
the giver and the givee.

Sharing erupts organically
out of the
richness of your life,
spilling over like hot,
brilliant lava –
into all you say and do.

Sharing opens your heart
and makes everything larger
than just you,
so you are not
the center of the universe . . .
not the end all and be all
of what you sow and reap.

Sharing expands your gratification.

It multiplies all that you do,

want to do and are capable

of doing.

It increases all that you have . . .

all that you are . . .

and all you enjoy.

Secret # 7

SERENDIPITY

*"I believe in Bach's Law which says,
'If anything can go right, it must!'"*

– Marcus Bach
The World of Serendipity

Serendipity is not
an accident . . .
it's not an occurrence.
It's a force that is released
when we liberate ourselves
from our *hidden shoulds*.

Serendipity . . .
keeps us *in the moment*
all the time
so we are responsive,
present and *alive* . . .
and therefore,
in touch with what
we are feeling . . .
so we can take action.

Dreams have passion . . .

Dreams have power . . .

Dreams are the starting point

of great things.

Trust what you know,
not what you see;
Trust your gut,
not your mind;
Trust yourself,
not what others say.

Facts are temporary
and situational . . .
they describe a present moment
observable reality.
But facts can change
. . . and reality can change too.

Be willing to be rich
before you are rich . . .
Be willing to be happy
before you have a reason to be.

Be willing to see, experience
and live what you *know*
to be true,
despite what the facts
tell you *seems* to be true.

Give yourself permission
to be rich, happy,
successful and healthy . . .
even though you do not
yet have what you need
to prove that you are.

Reach down deep inside you
to that place that
knows you are doing everything
you need to . . .
and that you already are and have
all that you desire.

Dare to Be
Joyful and Rich

"The riches you receive will be in exact proportion
to the definiteness of your vision, the fixity of your
purpose, the steadiness of your faith
and the depth of your gratitude."

– Wallace D. Wattles
The Science of Getting Rich

Abundance is not something
you have to create;
it is something you tap into.

Become quiet and still –
Feel the vibratory presence
of whatever it is you want . . .
and you will be led to it easily, naturally
and
effortlessly.

You are a co-creator
in the affluence
you experience,
the "riches" you enjoy . . .
with your attentiveness,
your responsiveness,
your decisiveness,
your visioning
and your belief.

What you do . . .
who you are every day –
is what you will experience
in your life.

You have to be willing
to *live* richly.
Joy and riches are not
attracted to those who don't . . .
and joy and riches
find those who do,
an irresistible magnet.

Thoughts on Living
With Joy and Riches

Money and love . . . joy and money . . . it's all the same. Whatever we do for joy, for love, for family and friends is the same thing we do for money.

It's all energy . . . It's all relationship . . . It's all just a dynamic – an interactivity.

The relationship between joy and riches reminds me of the relationship between beauty and utility. In ancient civilizations, beauty was not separated from the practicality, function or utility of a thing. Beauty was an intrinsic part of it . . . and never sacrificed for it. But, that's another book.

Over the centuries and in our modern culture, things of the soul and spirit seem to have been separated from the desires of our flesh. My prayer is that this book will help you bring them back together . . . to unite the longings of your soul with the desires of your flesh . . . so you get, claim and enjoy all the joy and riches you desire.

THE 7 SECRETS TO LIVING WITH JOY AND RICHES

Decide

Act

Believe

Be Grateful

Rejoice

Share

Serendipity

THE DARE

So, I dare you to . . .

Dare to be carefree

Dare to be free-spirited

Dare to trust what you know

Dare to be rich <u>before</u> you are rich

Dare to be delightfully, delectably,

deliciously rich . . .

Dare to be serendipitously rich!

About the Author

Madeleine Kay is the Best Selling Author of *Living Serendipitously* and *Serendipitously Rich*. Adventurist, unconventional success and motivational coach . . . and maverick entrepreneur, she has been featured in *Who's Who of American Women* and *Who's Who in the World*.

She speaks four languages, has been a resident of three continents, been a university instructor and international fashion model on two continents, ran her own advertising and marketing agency, wrote commentaries for the CBS affiliate in Miami and was even an actor in film, television and a music video.

Considered America's leading expert on *serendipity*, she combines the wisdom, passion and playfulness of serendipity sprinkled with her own unique brand of practical, down-to-earth common sense to help people get, claim and enjoy all the joy and riches they desire.

BOOKS BY MADELEINE KAY

Living Serendipitously . . . keeping the wonder alive

A lively and joyful read, *Living Serendipitously*, gets you to be an *active dreamer*, living your dreams, not just thinking about them. It captures the joyful essence of "the art of living" and shows you how to feel deliciously *alive*, vibrant and happy every day of your life . . . no matter what your circumstances. Einstein said, "There are only two ways to live your life – as though nothing is a miracle or as though *everything* is a miracle," *Living Serendipitously* aligns us with the *everything*.
(visit www.LivingSerendipitously.com or your favorite bookstore or online store.)

Living with Outrageous Joy

Joy is contagious . . . joy is revitalizing . . . joy is what every one of us wants to feel more of in our lives. This charming little gift book will re-ignite that feeling of joy in your life and your passion for living. Playfully inspiring and motivating, *Living with Outrageous Joy* will delight and revitalize you. It will open you up to the joy and adventure of living your life to the fullest every single day . . . unleashing in you that feeling of *aliveness* that so many of us are longing to feel.
(visit www.LivingWithOutrageousJoy.com or your favorite bookstore or online store.)

Serendipitously Rich . . . How to Get Delightfully,
Delectably, Deliciously Rich (or anything else you want)
in 7 Ridiculously Easy Steps

Changing "if" I am rich to "when" I am rich, has never
been simpler . . . or more fun. Refreshingly original,
and excitingly new, *Serendipitously Rich* will not only
motivate and inspire you – it will activate your "on"
switch, your "go" switch, your whatever it is that makes
you *do* something switch, so you can stop struggling and
start getting rich (and everything else you want) . . . with
effortless ease and unmitigated joy.
(visit www.SerendipitouslyRich.com or your favorite
bookstore or online store.)

Coming Soon

The UMM Factor . . .
(what you need in order to succeed)

This ground-breaking book about passion, purpose and
prosperity reveals the three things everyone must have in
order to succeed. Without all three, it is possible to succeed,
but not likely. With them – your success is guaranteed.
What are these three magical things? Madeleine Kay calls
them *The UMM Factor*.
(visit www.UmmFactor.com)

For information on *all* of Madeleine Kay's books, e-books, online courses, and events . . . go to www.madeleinekay.com

THE 7 SECRETS TO LIVING WITH JOY AND RICHES

Join our mailing list and receive a free *7 Myths About Money* mini e-course.

Visit the author at www.madeleinekay.com

NOTES ON JOY

NOTES ON JOY

DELICIOUSLY RICH NOTES

DELICIOUSLY RICH NOTES